# How to Preach the Gospel with Power:

## Practical and Spiritual Guidance from Initial Prayer to the Pulpit

By

Jonathan Anthony

# Copyright

© Copyright 2018 - All rights reserved.

The contents of this book may not be reproduced, duplicated or transmitted without direct written permission from the author. Under no circumstances will any legal responsibility or blame be held against the publisher for any reparation, damages, or monetary loss due to the information herein, either directly or indirectly.

Legal Notice:

This book is copyright protected. This is only for personal use. You cannot amend, distribute, sell, use, quote or paraphrase any part or the content within this book without the consent of the author.

Disclaimer Notice:

Please note the information contained within this document is for educational and entertainment purposes only. Every attempt has been made to provide accurate, up to date and reliable complete information. No warranties of any kind are expressed or implied. Readers acknowledge that the author is not engaging in the rendering of legal, financial, medical or professional advice. The content of this book has been derived from various sources. Please consult a licensed professional before attempting any techniques outlined in this book.

By reading this document, the reader agrees that under no circumstances is the author responsible for any losses, direct or indirect, which are incurred because of the use of information contained within this document, including, but not limited to, — errors, omissions, or inaccuracies.

All Scripture Quotations, unless otherwise indicated, are taken from the *New King James Version* or the *King James Version*.

# Acknowledgements

*To my Mom and Dad for introducing me to the greatest gift of all, relationship with Jesus Christ*

## Table of Contents

Copyright ................................................................. 2
Acknowledgements ................................................. 4
Introduction .............................................................. 8
Chapter 1 ................................................................ 15
The Foolishness of Preaching ............................... 15
Chapter 2 ................................................................ 23
What is the Gospel? .............................................. 23
   1. He Died ......................................................... 27
   He Rose Again .................................................. 28
Chapter 3 ................................................................ 30
When Kingdoms Collide ........................................ 30
   Kingdom Fundamentals .................................... 31
   The Problem – Sin ............................................ 33
   Rental Agreement ............................................. 33
Chapter 4 ................................................................ 37
The Undiluted Gospel. ........................................... 37
   Relevance .......................................................... 38
Chapter 5 ................................................................ 44
The Perfect Combination. ..................................... 44
   Why is this the case? ........................................ 48
Chapter 6 ................................................................ 52

You Get What You Preach ................................................... 52

Chapter 7 .............................................................................. 57

The Building of Faith by the Word. ................................... 57

Chapter 8 .............................................................................. 62

Preparation Stage .................................................................. 62

Chapter 9 .............................................................................. 68

Be Filled with the Spirit ....................................................... 68

Chapter 10 ............................................................................ 77

How can I be filled? ............................................................. 77

  What happens when I am filled with the Holy Spirit? 81

Chapter 11 ............................................................................ 87

The Power of Fasting ........................................................... 87

Chapter 12 ............................................................................ 96

Using the Spirit of God to Prepare what is to be delivered .. 96

  As you write. ................................................................. 101

  A Glimpse of the Gifts ................................................. 103

Chapter 13 .......................................................................... 104

Preach it – Delivery ........................................................... 104

  Practical. ....................................................................... 105

  Spiritual ......................................................................... 107

Chapter 14 .......................................................................... 111

Moving in the Holy Ghost ................................................. 111

  Right and Left .............................................................. 112

  Division of Aaron (Left). ............................................. 117

    The Division of Joshua (Right) ........................................... 119

    Hints of the spirit ............................................................ 122

Chapter 14 ............................................................................ 126

Conclusion ............................................................................ 126

Bonus .................................................................................. 129

## Introduction

So, I sat there completely transfixed. I couldn't take my eyes off him. Every word he spoke shook my small body and caused me to lose myself in the stories he was telling. I must have been no older than 8. I listened to this Preacher, as he began to tell of experiences he'd had in other countries, preaching in old fashioned canvas tents, something that I had never experienced.

He told of seeing people shaken to their core by the power of the word. His rhetoric caused me to imagine him standing, mid flow, white shirted, drenched with sweat, handkerchief in hand, pointlessly wiping his sodden brow, clinging onto this microphone as though it was in danger of escaping.

He told of how unsaved women had stood there listening, with their backs to the canvas, shaking their heads side to side violently with conviction, yet at the same time being powerfully overcome by the love of God being preached. He said, so dramatic where their head shakes that their tear drops would reach the canvas behind them, until so heavy was the presence of God upon them, they ran to the altar in repentance.

He told the story of their husbands; full of anger due to the sudden conversion of their wives; now charging up the middle isle of the tent, fists clenched, ready to attack the preacher. He then told of these very men falling short of their target as they hit the ground due to the power of God in the place.

And at that moment I made up my mind that I wanted to be a Preacher of the Gospel. I wanted to allow God to move through me in such a way that people's lives would be changed forever. I wanted to be an oracle God, His mouthpiece, I wanted to be him here speaking to His people, a vessel he could rely upon like the prophets of old.

That was many years ago, and if I look back and then forward I don't believe that there are many preachers like that anymore. There aren't as many tent missions, nor preachers that would preach until their back is drenched wet with sweat.

I vividly remember sitting there as a young boy, listening as preachers would come through my small church in Rugby. I would be hoping and wishing that the gaze of the preacher wouldn't fall on me, just in case he knew what I was thinking through the Gifts of the Spirit. Not that I was thinking anything evil, but I just didn't want them to know that I was tired, or more interested in watching the football afterwards. With the preacher came a holy reverence.

Fading are the days when we would hear a preacher declare a sermon with that mystic preaching intonation, sharing the gospel in such a way that could pierce a soul yet heal it with one stroke of that two-edged sword.

Nowadays preaching really isn't called preaching anymore. In most cases it has been replaced by the word "**Address**" or it's a "strong explanation of an opinion". Some ministers have a style which is more conversational, almost to the point where it would be acceptable for someone to disagree with what is being said at the time of their sermon. This being acceptable because the content of their address is so mixed up with human opinion that the word of God is of no effect. It's like diluted fruit juice.

I have written this book not condemn any specific style of word declaration, but to highlight the fact that **preaching** the gospel, is still important. Discussing the gospel and sharing the gospel are all good however, there is still place for the dynamic, authoritative, powerful declaration of the Word of God through preaching.

In this book we will look at how this can still be done, and how it can still be effective even in this generation. From background research I have found that it is rare now that mentors (if they are in place) ever really train mentees on "how to preach" and this book is also designed to fill this void.

Whether you are a quiet preacher, a loud preacher, a demonstrative preacher, a general sharer of the gospel, or you are just trying to change and shift the way you minister, I pray that this book will bless you.

All this being said, the most important aspect is the anointing. Without the anointing it really doesn't matter what style you share the word of God with, you will just be lecturing.

The Bible is quite clear concerning this matter and states the following:

> Isaiah 10:27
> It shall come to pass in that day
> That his burden will be taken away from your shoulder,
> And his yoke from your neck,
> **And the yoke will be destroyed because of the anointing oil.**

I have been preaching now for over 20 years. Having started preaching in my home in a small house group in the Midlands. I have now had the wonderful opportunity to share this wonderful gospel across multiple continents, to different tribes and races.

In this book I have shared with you all the key elements that I have learnt throughout my journey. We will get very practical as well as very spiritual. I will also challenge a few areas of thinking. So be prepared. We will look at everything from one's initial preparation through to what happens post sermon, including guidance in operating under the anointing of God in an altar call scenario.

In the New Testament we see quite clearly that every time a message is preached something happens. Therefore, by the end of this book, when you preach, it is my prayer that you will expect something to happen. Why? Well because you will have preached the Kingdom of God and by faith I believe it would have manifested itself wherever you delivered it.

So, come with me as we learn **How to Preach the Gospel with Power.**

# 1
## The Foolishness of Preaching

### Mark 1:13

*The voice of one crying in the wilderness, Prepare ye the way of the Lord, make his paths straight.*

"Here you go son, it's your go!"

I had been leading up to this point for what had felt like my whole life.

Having been brought up in a Pentecostal Church I had been listening to your stereotypical fiery preacher, every Sunday, for 16 years. Now this was my opportunity. For the first time I was being asked to lift my voice in a busy city centre and nail my colours to the mast by declaring who I believed in, why believed in him and then conclude by explaining why they should also.

My heart was beating out of my chest and I am sure my hand was also shaking as I held the microphone for the first time. I had no Bible with me, just the words that had *"been hidden within my heart, that I might not sin against him"* (*Psalms 119:11*).

Then I heard myself shout out through the microphone, "Bilston, I don't come to you in my name alone, but I come to you in the name of the Lord Jesus Christ..."

It is at times like this that you either have it, or you don't have it. I thank God that he was with me as I preached the Gospel in the town centre that brisk Saturday morning. Many would have looked at me and thought me a fool. I **heard** others laugh and scoff as I delivered what I had. I am sure people looked at me as a young man that had been brainwashed by these so-called Christians. But all I know was that inside of me that day was a fire burning (mixed with an adrenaline and nervousness).

I am sure I looked like a fool to anyone who didn't understand. But for the first time I realised what the foolishness of preaching was.

So, the question must be asked, why does God choose the foolishness of preaching as the avenue for us to declare His message to the world?

I submit that the answer to this question is very simple. It is because **preaching to this world system is still foolish.**

This is especially true in a religious sense. People are used to charismatic people standing in great theatres or even declaring their point of view in parliament or at the Senate. These people are preaching! Our politicians preach to each other in parliament, comedians preach to their audiences at the Albert Hall. But when it comes to declaring truth, somehow in the religious social arena, which is very clean cut, traditional and straight, the crazy extrovert preacher comes across as **"out of order"**.

1 Corinthians 1:27 states *"But God hath chosen the foolish things of the world to confound the wise; and God hath chosen the weak things of the world to confound the things which are mighty"*

Preaching is the perfect example of this scripture being satisfied.

The Bible states in Isaiah 55:8&9

*"For my thoughts are not your thoughts,*
*neither are your ways my ways,"*
*declares the Lord.*
*"As the heavens are higher than the earth,*
*so are my ways higher than your ways*

*and my thoughts than your thoughts*. (NKJV)

God does not think as we think. He makes it very clear in this scripture.

Therefore, if God can take that which the world classes as foolish and use it as something to bring glory to His name; theoretically the preacher doesn't get the glory, God does.

We've all seen the crazy preachers on the television jumping and screaming, preaching down the aisles, preaching on top of tables, standing on chairs declaring that "you must be saved". Generally, anyone who sees this would class it as foolish.

And it still causes me to wonder why God would choose such an avenue? An avenue that I am sure many have laughed at, scoffed at, and despised. But he has chosen it and through it we have seen millions receive what he has allowed to flow through it.

When you think of the revivals across the last 30 years in Ethiopia, the Philippines and major parts of South America, it was a man/woman that used the vehicle of "foolish preaching" who created a spiritual platform for people to be saved, healed and delivered.

**Question: Why does God choose the foolishness of preaching?**
**Answer: It's so that only He gets the glory.**

We see this behavioural pattern of God recorded throughout the whole of the Bible, choosing that which we as humans think is ridiculous to bring glory to his name.

David, just a mere shepherd boy looking after his father's sheep, when the prophet Samuel came to the house of Jesse, David wasn't even in the mind of his father. He was insignificant and the thought of David potentially being king was probably seen as a foolish one. Jesse lined up all his sons in front of the prophet in the hope that one of the strong, strapping, young men would be called to be leader of the nation. But God had other plans. It was the young skinny stick of a lad in the field that had caught the attention of the Lord. The one that others felt was insignificant. David, the brother that others didn't see as an element that mattered; it was he that God chose to elevate and use.

We remember Gideon hiding behind the wine press complaining to God about how things had been. A spiritual weakling only a fool would choose him. But look what God did in the life of this man.

Even in the Gospel of John we see an adulterous woman sat by the well. She has a meeting with the man Christ Jesus and subsequently brings a whole town to meet the God-man, our saviour Jesus Christ. I put it to you that God chooses the foolishness of preaching to confound us and to help us to understand that without him we can do nothing.

Lastly, John the Baptist, preaching in the desert and clothed in camel's hair, is still known to be the greatest preacher that ever lived. Even though he looked foolish he preached a message that would change the world.

That is why God choses the foolishness of preaching, because only the foolishness of it brings glory to His name and lifts Him up. And the word of God states that if "he be lifted up then he will draw all men unto himself (John 12:32)."

So, don't worry about how it looks when you declare the word. Don't be afraid of how you sound, if you get over excited. God has chosen this way of declaring the word to bring glory to Himself. So, preach it with everything you have!

# 2
# What is the Gospel?

*By this gospel you are saved, if you hold firmly to the word I preached to you. Otherwise, you have believed in vain. For what I received I passed on to you as of first importance: that Christ died for our sins according to the Scriptures, that he was buried, that he was raised on the third day according to the Scriptures*

1 Corinthians 15:2-4

The word gospel is used repeatedly in the Scripture. It is also used countless times every weekend by preachers across this globe. But what is the gospel?

The gospel in the translation of the Greek noun basically means **"good news"**. Therefore, theoretically anything that is seen as good news could be classified as "gospel". The old English 'godspel' came from the two words 'good' and 'spell' coming from the word "story" or "news". Therefore, godspel is a good story.

Gospel is also the translation of the Greek noun **euangelion** and it occurs 76 times in the New Testament. The verb **euangelizo** occurs 54 times and it basically means "to bring or announce good news".

Are you still with me?

Both words come from the noun 'angelos' which means "messenger". To truly understand the meaning of this word we must look at the classical Greek. Here there was actually someone called the Euangelos. The Euangelos was one who brought a message of victory, political or personal, that caused joy to come to the people.

Both the verbs and nouns from this derivative are used repeatedly throughout scripture to cause the Christian reading the Bible to understand the importance of what is taking place in their life. The word 'gospel' is also there to announce to mankind that there is victory through this good news, the Kingdom of God is at hand. Lastly, the word 'gospel' and its derivatives are still there to proclaim that the death, burial and resurrection of Jesus Christ offer new life to those who believe.

The Wycliff Bible puts it this way:

*"the central truth of the gospel is that God has provided a way of salvation for men through the gift of his son Jesus Christ to the world. He suffered as a sacrifice for sin, overcame death, and now offers to share in his triumph to all who will accept it." This is the gospel. The gospel is good news because it*

*is a gift of God, not something that must be earned by pennants or self-improvement emanating from oneself. But it is good news because it is from God.*

Paul puts it another way in 1 Corinthians 15:1-5

*"Moreover, brethren, I declare unto you the gospel which I preached unto you, which also ye have received, and wherein ye stand; By which also ye are saved, if ye keep in memory what I preached unto you, unless ye have believed in vain. For I delivered unto you first of all that which I also received, how that Christ died for our sins according to the scriptures; And that he was buried, and that he rose again the third day according to the scriptures: And that he was seen of Cephas, then of the twelve".*

This is simply Paul's summary of what we call **the gospel**.

Let me for a few moments break it down into two aspects.

　　1. He Died

When Jesus died he paid the penalty for sin. If you are reading this book I will assume that you know why. If not let me remind you anyway.

Romans 6:23a
*For the wages of sin is death;*

And what was worse was…

Romans 3:23
*…all have sinned, and come short of the glory of God;*

And alas;

Hebrews 9:22
*…* **without shedding of blood there is no remission.**

Therefore, when Christ died that wage or penalty was satisfied. But the second aspect of this gospel is that **he rose again**.

## 2. He Rose Again

It is because he rose again that we can now overcome the power of sin and death. When he arose, he conquered death which is why we read the following scripture so often at funerals.

1 Corinthians 15:55
*O death, where is thy sting? O grave, where is thy victory?*

The gospel is the fact that Jesus paid the price for your life and mine. Not only are we free from sin, but we are also not subject to the power of death.

This all being said, I would submit that the Gospel of Salvation is just an element of God's Gospel to the world. I suggest this on the basis that when Christ walked the earth he also preached **the Gospel of the Kingdom.**

It is only when one understands all elements of God's gospel message found in Matthew, Mark, Luke and John that as a preacher of the gospel you can deliver a true reflection of what Christ wants for His church. It is not enough just to preach the Gospel of Salvation 100% of the time. As a preacher it is also your duty to explain what the responder to this gospel has been brought into. The answer to this is clearly... the Kingdom of God.

This short excerpt from my book When Kingdoms Collide brings clarity to this point. See you on the other side.

## 3

## When Kingdoms Collide

The Kingdom of God is real. It is not a figment of our imagination. It is not a fairy story made up at some point in human history, nor is it a concept used by God to help us understand something else. The Kingdom of God is as real as you or I.

Using the same analogy that Jesus uses in John 3:8, something does not have to be visible for us to know that it exists. As true as the wind that blows across the ocean, so is the Kingdom of God to you and me.

This Kingdom of God is as real as the cross of Calvary. It's as real as the blood that ran down the body of our saviour Jesus Christ. It is as real as the resurrection on the third day and his ascension into glory.

The Kingdom of God is as real as the Baptism of the Holy Ghost and speaking with other tongues. Lastly, the Kingdom of God is accessible right now even as you read this short book

## Kingdom Fundamentals

For us to understand the Kingdom of God we need to form a foundation. Paul says in writing to the Romans;

Romans 1:20
*For the invisible things of him from the creation of the world are clearly seen, being understood by the things that are made, even his eternal power and Godhead*

So here goes…

Any Kingdom is ruled by a King (monarch), which is why it is called a King-dom.

Therefore…The Kingdom of God is ruled by The King. That King is God. God's name is Jesus. (John 5:43)

The bible is about a kingdom and about a country. In our case the country/territory is called earth.

The bible is about a colonisation project where the king tries to extend his influence on a different territory (earth). In our situation the King (God) was trying to extend his influence over the earth.

God wanted to make earth a colony of heaven. This is the project of the bible. His interest isn't to get you to heaven. Essentially, your spirit and soul are not from earth they are directly from God. Therefore, when you are born again you are born from His world to operate in this world. You were sent to colonise earth for heaven.

God wanted to extend the Kingdom of Heaven to earth bringing His invisible kingdom to visible earth.

The Problem – Sin

With these fundamentals in mind we can now look to truly understand what happened when Adam and Eve sinned in the Garden of Eden.

Essentially the colony declared independence from the Kingdom of God. Mankind in its wisdom stated, "We can do this on our own". Therefore, the bible is about redemption and about the recolonization of the earth. God's Kingdom coming again.

This is what it is all about. Not understanding the general plan of God means that we come from the wrong perspective when we approach Christian living, prayer and Christianity as a whole.

Let's continue…

Rental Agreement

When God created the world, it was almost like the owner of a property giving the keys of that property to the tenant. In this case, God (Landlord) gave mankind (Tenant) the keys to the earth, telling us to be fruitful and multiply and have dominion (Genesis 1:26). However, as we all know by disobeying God and eating of the forbidden tree we (mankind) gave the keys, dominion and all ownership away when we obeyed Satan and sin entered in.

Once again taking up the colonial analogy, when this happened the colony (earth) declared independence from the Kingdom of God. So, the bible is about redemption and the re-colonisation of the earth by the Kingdom of God. It's about the Kingdom of God taking back ownership of the earth.

When we understand this, we can now completely understand what the cross of Calvary is about. The removal and washing away of sin so that the King of Kings can once again have dominion in our life. With this revelation we can now understand what the blood is about. It reconciles creation to its maker.

Understanding the adage of colonisation will help you understand exactly what happens on a day to day basis in your home and in your churches or wherever you feel the presence of God. What you are feeling when you pray is the actual presence of the Kingdom of God rising in that specific place.

Remember, history gives us in-depth detail about how colonisation worked. We have many different examples to learn from. For example, the British colonised Jamaica and parts of Asia. The French colonised countries such as Haiti. The Spanish colonised Cuba and this list goes on. These were all Kingdoms that were looking to spread their culture and influence across the world and this is what God has always looked to do with his glory. When you are praying "Thy Kingdom Come", you are praying something powerful.

In concluding, now we understand how the **gospel of salvation** fits like a glove into the **gospel of the kingdom**. Now the preaching of Christ throughout Matthew, Mark, Luke and John should make complete sense.

Reader, it is this gospel that he preached, it is this gospel that the Apostles preached, and it is this gospel that you were born and called preach.

I challenge you the next time you stand behind a pulpit to think about all those that have preach this message before you. In a world where it is more fashionable to prepare a sermon that is ear tickling and relevant, it is the message of the cross that is still the most powerful and has the gravitas to save a lost soul, pulling them from the fire (Jude 1:23) and setting them upon the solid rock.

# 4
## The Undiluted Gospel.

We live in an age where the gospel of God in many cases has been completely diluted. It is therefore our responsibility, every time we stand behind a pulpit to make sure we bring theongregation back to our roots in the word of God. In the "adjusted" words of the American judicial system;

*"We swear to preach the truth, the whole truth, and nothing but the truth".*

Why? Because it is the truth that makes us free (John 8:32). Note, it doesn't just make **you** free, but everyone within the sound of your voice, listening live, listening to a recording in the car, on a podcast, on a radio station, whoever listens to the word you declare, if it is soaked in the primary source of the gospel, it will make them free also. Selah

Theoretically, this means that someone could be listening to one of your sermons in 100 years' time and because its soaked in the truth it could set them free, right there on Mars! (Joke!)

Even as you read this book you have a decision to make, will you be a passive preacher of the gospel or will you be a proactive preacher of the gospel. Will you grab a hold of what God has given through his mighty word and will you run the race that has been set before you? Or will you go the broad way of the crowd?

Relevance

One of the biggest obstacles that we have in this age is that of relevance. Unfortunately for some, in looking to be relevant it is easy for them to become destructive and forget the roots of the message that they have been called to preach. Instead of a message from God, they have a "Chinese whispers" message.

Please follow me for a moment.

The Bible states in John 10:10
*"The thief cometh not, but for to steal, and to kill, and to destroy"*

The actuality of this statement is that Satan will do everything he can in the life of the Christian to get them to misunderstand or to misinterpret what God has done for them and therefore leave the Christian to live a life short of what God has already paid the price for.

Preacher, God wants you to preach the whole gospel. Preacher, God wants you to live the whole gospel.

That being said, the enemy would have you live a Christian life at 30% when God wants you to live it at 100%. And therefore, Satan's plan is to nullify the word of God in your life and in the lives of others without us even knowing it. He calls Christians to compromise this gospel of God that was purchased by him at Calvary.

One of the biggest threats of our age is individuals misunderstanding the power of the gospel believing that the only use that it has is to get sinners into heaven. I would controversially submit that preaching the gospel of salvation **alone** chops the legs off revival. Nevertheless, preaching salvation along with what we are called unto, puts legs on revival and allows it to run for generations.

A compromised gospel leads to a powerless church. And so, Satan looks to sell the lie to the flesh of the Christian that is okay being average. He whispers into the ear of the Christian that certain aspects of the gospel preached by the Apostles are no longer relevant.

Lies such as; speaking with tongues is no longer essential, that the infilling of the Holy Spirit is no longer an aspect that is called for, but just for a show and a chosen few. Satan will sow the seed that holiness before God no longer matters, that sharing my faith is something that is not important and that giving to God of my tithes and offerings is no longer relevant and will not influence my own finances.

Subsequently, because there are aspects of these beliefs that are extremely easy for us to accept, and so the Christian accepts them thus diluting the original message of the gospel preached in the book of Acts. The result of this is that gospel of this time, in many cases, has **no power**, because in some areas of Christendom it is not the **same gospel** that was preached by the apostles of old.

Why? Because it has been diluted by the world system, the cosmos, this worldly way of thinking.

But all is not lost. I believe that the reason that you are reading this book is because you have a desire not just to lecture from the pulpit but to declare and to preach with power the gospel that was preached by the Apostles of old. The same power that followed Peter and John at the Gate beautiful is the same power that you are wanting in your life right here, right now. And so, my encouragement to you is to get back to the basics of the apostolic belief system because what was preached in that time was surely the gospel of God.

Romans 1:1 states that there was a "gospel of God". And it was this gospel that Paul preached. It was not the gospel of man or the gospel of half God and half man. It was the gospel of God.

And even though not flashy, or entertaining, the gospel of God is still powerful.

Let me remind you of some of its basics.

The gospel of God still says even though you and I were born in sin shaped in iniquity (Psalm 51:1), God loved the world that he gave his only begotten son that whosoever believes in him should not perish but have eternal life (John 3:16). The gospel of God still states that with him all things are possible (Matthew 19:26). The gospel of God still states the signs shall follow them that believe (Mark 16:17). So, before you move on to the next chapter I encourage you to analyse your life, analyse your sermons. Review what you deliver to the people you are responsible for. Then ask yourself the question; Is it the gospel of God, or is it your gospel that originates from you? Selah.

# 5
## The Perfect Combination.

The gospel shouts from the mountain tops;

**"It doesn't have to be this way, I have made a way of escape, you don't have to die you can have life and have it more abundantly".**

As previously referred to, the gospel is all about telling and sharing.

While I was studying to write this book there was however something that jumped out at me again and again as I read the word gospel.

See if you can see what it is:

Matthew 4:23 and Jesus went about all Galilee, teaching in their synagogues, and **preaching** the gospel of the kingdom, and hearing all manner of sickness and all manner of disease among the people.

Matthew 9:35 and Jesus went about all the cities and villages, teaching in their synagogues, and **preaching** the gospel of the kingdom, and healing every sickness and every disease among the people.

Matthew 11:5 the blind receive their sight, and the lame walk, the lepers are cleansed, and the deaf hear, the dead are raised up, and the poor have the gospel **preached** to them.

Matthew 24:14 and this gospel of the kingdom shall be **preached** in all the world for a witness unto all nations; and then shall the end come.

Mark 1:14 – 15 now after that John was put in prison, Jesus came into Galilee, **preaching** the gospel of the kingdom. And saying the time is fulfilled, and the kingdom of God is at hand: repent he and believe the gospel.

Luke 4:18 the spirit of the Lord is upon me, because she had anointed me to **preach** the gospel to the poor;

And we could go on.

The word that should ring true to you in all these passages of scripture are the words "preach" or "preached".

The Greek word for preach is "euaggelizo".

It means to herald, to proclaim or to publish.

For me this makes everything very simple. Once one has tasted and seen that the gospel is real.

More specifically, once someone has tasted and seen that God is good, I believe that it is time for them to tell the world! Putting it simply, it's time for them to preach. We all remember the old Sunday school song, "this little light of mine I am going to let it shine". Well then, it is time for us to do as the song says. "Go tell it on the mountain over the hills and everywhere" that this gospel is real.

Friend, it is time for you to declare it from your pulpit and declare it out from every aspect of your life.

Now I cannot help but think of the famous duos or pairs in life. I'm thinking of Batman and Robin, Morecambe and Wise even the Chuckle Brothers. If we are talking about pairs around food; salt-and-pepper, macaroni and cheese, chips and gravy (I'm making myself hungry). The same way all these things are best together so it is with the words **Gospel** and **Preach**.

We have just read it numerous amounts of times; **the gospel must be preached**. When the gospel is served on the plate of preaching history suggest it is here that it has its most astounding affects.

It was the preaching of the gospel by Peter that brought revival in Jerusalem in Acts 2. It was the preaching of the gospel by Philip a few chapters later that brought revival to Samaria. It was the publishing of the gospel by Peter in Acts 10 at the house of Cornelius that brought the outpouring of the Spirit of God in that righteous man's house. All these examples strongly point to the fact that for the gospel to be effective it must be declared.

Why is this the case?

The Bible is clear concerning this. My father would say that "the currency of heaven is faith". And the way faith comes is by hearing and hearing by the word (Romans 10:17).

Therefore, when I **hear** the word it is easier for me to digest than when I just think it. Why? Because faith cometh by hearing and not just thinking.

Now, you may be reading this thinking that you are not confident enough to preach and declare so that people can **hear**. But I submit to you that that's not the case. For we were **all** called to be preachers as soon as we are saved. The book of Mark 16:15 is clear and states:

*"And he said unto them, go ye into all the world, and preach the gospel to every creature".*

Even in Acts 1:8 it says, *but ye shall receive power, after that the Holy Ghost is come upon you: and ye shall be witnesses.* Yes, witnesses i.e. preachers of the gospel. He doesn't fill us with power, dynamite, to sit around, play church and enjoy being in the pews keeping our traditions. The reason that you are endued with power from on high is to be able to declare and to be counted a witness of the things of God.

1 Corinthians 1:21 puts it this way. *For after that in the wisdom of God the world by wisdom knew not God, it pleased God by the foolishness of preaching to save them that believe.*

It's time for us to declare the word of God that will in turn cause faith in the hearts of men to grow again. It is upon this platform of faith that God comes to dwell in the lives of men. You are a publisher of what God has done for you through his gospel. Born-again, saved by grace and transformed through the power of the Holy Spirit. This is the effect of the preaching of the gospel and it still is, whether you preach it, or TD Jakes preaches it. Same God, same word.

I challenge you today, if you are not seeing God move then stop sharing and start preaching and declaring the facts that God has already done. Let the gospel be served up on the platform of faith and see what God can do in your life.

## 6

## You Get What You Preach

There is an old preacher's saying, "you get what you preach".

If I preach baptism, then after a while I will get baptism. If I preach salvation, then after a while I will see people saved.

In my own life even at a young age when I preached faith, and acted **by** faith, as a result I saw God do miraculous things. You can experience the same, just believe and trust the word of God.

There was a period in my life when God was teaching me to trust him in ministry. I've never been entirely confident in terms of pulpit ministry because I never thought I was good enough both technically and spiritually to have God move through me in the way that I desired. So, when I saw it begin to happen it completely blew me away. Interestingly, it happened when I began to step out in faith and leave opportunity for God to do what only he could do.

This firstly came in the opportunities presented themselves to pray for people to receive the baptism of the Holy Spirit with the evidence of speaking with other tongues. Before I begin to illustrate my point, the aim of this book is not to have a debate about the initial evidence of speaking in tongues and the gift of tongues, my point is only that at the time churches that I would evangelise in across Europe were hungry for people to be baptised with the Holy Ghost in the way that they were in Acts 2.

Whilst praying for people I found that over time I got into a pattern. I would preach about the need for the infilling of the Spirit. I would build my case around book of Acts. I would talk about the life of Peter before and after Pentecost. Then I would call people to the front and asked them whether they would like to receive the same baptism of the Holy Spirit with evidence of speaking with tongues that Peter had.

Let us be extremely practical here, there was no guarantee anything was going to happen physically speaking. And yes, it was highly likely that if God didn't turn up then I would look like a false prophet. But by this time, in my life I had had enough of talking about things and not seeing them happen. I was prepared to go for it!

Back to the altar call. I would then talk about the need for repentance and based upon the word of God explain that sin needed to be forgiven. I would quote the scriptures that state *without the shedding of blood there was no remission of sin (Hebrews 9:22)*, and state that *it is not as will that any should perish but the all should come to repentance (2 Peter 3:9)*. And then I would teach them to worship and to open their mouths and declare thanks and praise to God. I would say that *"with our mouths we confess"* and *"out of the mouth the heart speaks" (Luke 6:45)*.

I would then have them count to three and shout "hallelujah!" I would explain that sometimes this word would mean 10,000 praises to God. People would shout and reach out to the Lord, and even when they would do it on a practice run, I could feel the atmosphere change because they would be publishing, heralding, praises to God.

I would then say, "we're going to do for real" and prepare them by saying "at the next shout of hallelujah, the Spirit of God will take hold of your tongue and you will speak in another language".

With this principle based on pure faith, I saw God move in some amazing ways over that period and even now I still see people received the Holy Ghost in this way.

I have seen individuals receive it this way in their homes, on the streets and in church meetings. But it took faith. Faith on my part to leave a gap for God to move based upon the word that I had preached.

At some point, if you truly want to be used by God you really must take a step of faith and implement what you've preached. Allowing those that you have preached to to respond to the word that you've given.

Build faith and then let God do what only he can.

# 7
## The Building of Faith by the Word.

Romans 10:17
*So then Faith cometh by hearing and hearing by the word.*

Hebrews 11:6
*But without faith it is impossible to please Him, for he who comes to God must believe that He is, and that He is a rewarder of those who diligently seek Him.*

When I first started preaching, I was told that it was important to share stories of the moving of God for it was that which would build faith in those that were listening to me.

The issue that I had however, was that at the age of 16, I didn't have many stories, because I hadn't lived very long. So, in the light of this I would listen to preaching from other ministers and then share their stories to build faith.

When preaching about the importance of relationship with God, I would retell a story of an old preacher who feel down dead in a busy airport in Australia. He had suffered a heart attack. They tried all they could, but they couldn't resuscitate him. The ministers that he was with continued to pray even after people had given up, but it was felt as though all hope was lost. Then miraculously, whilst in the ambulance his heart started to beat again. After several weeks, the doctors were amazed at his recovery. They couldn't understand why he had survived such a major incidence. The old preacher called them across to his bedside and asked whether they had heard of a man called Jesus of Nazareth. They tried to dismiss him, but he asked again. They agreed together that they had heard of him. The old preacher stated, "well that's the difference then, you have heard about him, but I know him".

This story would drum home the need to know God and not just to know **about** him.

I was very careful not to come across as though it was my experience when I told stories and I would encourage you to do the same. One would never want dishonesty to prevent God moving through you.

I'd start by saying "there was a preacher that…" or "There was a man that…" I would then continue to tell the story and back it up with a scriptural reference. The aim was always to build faith in God for that very instant.

If I was to put it practically it would be done as follows:

1. Make Preaching Point
2. Back it Up with Scripture
3. Give scriptural evidence through a bible story
4. Give a working example from personal story or one I had heard.

It was through this way of preaching that I managed to bring the word of God into the here and now. God would make people hungry for what was spoken through this way of preaching the gospel.

As you prepare your next sermon I challenge you to use this four-step principle. In addition to this I would encourage you to look to answer the following two questions?

1. What do I want God to do in the lives of the listener?
2. How am I feeding His people today?

# 8
## Preparation Stage

If you haven't got a prayer life, then I would almost go as far as to say you should forget about preaching if you don't plan to change.

It is through your prayer that you allow your spirit to become receptive in preparation for the seed of the word to be planted inside your spirit. Whatever the message may be, it needs to mean something to you.

I'm a dad and I have three young children. I have found that I can't start preparing for a message straight away with no preplanning of when, and where I will start addressing my sermon. I.e. I cannot just sit down randomly at my computer and write my sermon straight of the bat. This is because at any given time I have so many issues that are going through my head. (Can I get an amen all you dads out there)

Thoughts such as, who needs to be where? who needs to go and do what? Money, Management, Church, and the list goes on. Therefore, I find that once I set aside a time to prepare I look to start from the basis of prayer. I find that a period of prayer really focuses the mind.

I encourage you to go to prayer with a notepad so that you can write down the things God impresses on your heart. If there have been topics that you have mediated on before this prayer time, I encourage you to write them down and then allow God to develop those points as you pray. For some people they may receive pictures, for others they will say something in prayer and that statement will trigger other areas that God wants to be brought to the attention of his people.

Now, I have never been one of those *"I was walking down the street and God said to me"* people. But God does speak to me with strong impressions. And I do believe that he speaks to many people in this way. So, as you pray allow your mind to wonder concerning the things of him. Trust your spirit as it communes with the Spirit of God. And see what he would say unto you.

In some cases, you may find that the Spirit of God comes upon you and you begin to write almost unnaturally. I.e. with the speed that would be uncommon. It almost feels as though you are writing/typing under the influence of the Spirit of God. If this spirit comes upon you keep writing until it lifts.

A sermon that would take four hours to scribe, all of a sudden could 30 minutes because you are writing your heart that is aligned with the heart of God. For many years this would happen to me as I prepared my sermons. It was almost as though the Spirit of

God would come upon me as he did when the fathers of old wrote the Bible. Now, I am in no way saying that my sermons are to be held in at the same level as the bible. I am just saying that when you prepare your message you can do so under the influence of the Spirit of God.

Sometimes I would feel the presence of God on me so strongly that I would cry over my laptop, I would pace the floor speaking with tongues because I would really feel the heart of God concerning what I would be sharing. It was almost as though God was preaching it to my heart before I preached it to His people.

There is no greater aid to writing your sermon than the Holy Ghost. I would go as far as to say that before you write your next sermon make sure you have been filled with the Holy Spirit.

The Bible is clear without him we can do nothing. And I would rather take the example of Peter preaching the gospel in the book of Acts **full** of the Holy Spirit than just going in my own strength.

Preacher, the infilling of the Holy Spirit is for you. FACT.

I would go as far as to say that if you're reading this book, it is for you TODAY.

*For the promise is unto you, and to your children, and to all that are afar off, even as many as the Lord our God shall call. Acts 2:39*

I feel that the infilling of the Holy Spirit is so important for the preacher that for the next few pages we will look at the subject in detail and show you how you can receive it even as you read this book. You can then take the principles from this book and use them in your own ministry.

So now, let's take a hold of Psalms 139:23, "*Search me oh Lord and know my heart*". Right now, if you have not yet received the Holy Spirit with the evidence of speaking with tongues, I encourage you to put your pride to the side and let the Scripture to lead you. Why? Because receiving the baptism of the Holy Spirit will be the greatest boost your preaching will ever have. You want to preach the gospel with power? Be prepared to receive the dynamite that drives it all.

# 9
## Be Filled with the Spirit

Here we go again, I am heading back to the book of Acts. The place where the church started over 2000 years ago. Here we hear the cry from the masses verse 37 of chapter 2

*"Now when they heard this, they were pricked in their heart, and said unto Peter and to the rest of the apostles, Men and brethren, what shall we do?"*

So, the Apostle Peter responds to them,

*"Repent, and be baptized every one of you in the name of Jesus Christ for the remission of sins, and ye shall receive the gift of the Holy Ghost". (Acts 2:38 KJV)*

The first thing for the believer to understand is that this promise of being baptised with the holy spirit is to **you and your children**. It is not for a select few. It is for you preacher, so go for it. Go search for it. Go do what it takes to receive it. Stop living a life short of what was purchased for you and sent as a gift so that you can fulfil your call properly.

Am I condemning believers that have not yet had an Acts 2 experience? NO. Am I saying that if you haven't received the Holy Spirit, every message that you have preached before this point has been based in the flesh? NO. But what I am saying is that God wants us to have the fullness. There is more. Look at this clear example in Acts 19 when the Apostle Paul comes across some disciples of John.

*And it came to pass, that, while Apollos was at Corinth, Paul having passed through the upper coasts came to Ephesus: and finding certain disciples,*

*He said unto them, Have ye received the Holy Ghost since ye believed? And they said unto him, We have not so much as heard whether there be any Holy Ghost.*

*And he said unto them, Unto what then were ye baptized? And they said, Unto John's baptism.*

*Then said Paul, John verily baptized with the baptism of repentance, saying unto the people, that they should believe on him which should come after him, that is, on Christ Jesus.*

*When they heard this, they were baptized in the name of the Lord Jesus.*

***And when Paul had laid his hands upon them, the Holy Ghost came on them; and they spake with tongues, and prophesied.***
*Acts 19:1-6*

My question to you is very simple. Have you received the Holy Spirit since you became a Christian? If not, why not? If all those reasons you have given yourself are invalid, which am sure they are, it's time for you to be filled with the Holy Spirit. Look inside the scriptures and honestly tell me that God does not want you to be filled…

*Jesus answered and said unto him, Verily, verily, I say unto thee, Except a man be born again, he cannot see the kingdom of God.*
*John 3:3*

*Jesus answered, Verily, verily, I say unto thee, Except a man be born of water and of the Spirit, he cannot enter into the kingdom of God.*
*John 3:5*

*I indeed baptize you with water unto repentance. but he that cometh after me is mightier than I, whose shoes I am not worthy to bear: he shall baptize you with the Holy Ghost, and with fire:*

*Matthew 3:11*

*He that believeth on me, as the scripture hath said, out of his belly shall flow rivers of living water.*
*John 7:38*

*Howbeit when he, the Spirit of truth, is come, he will guide you into all truth: for he shall not speak of himself; but whatsoever he shall hear, that shall he speak: and he will shew you things to come.*
*John 16:13*

*And be not drunk with wine, wherein is excess; but be filled with the Spirit;*
*Ephesians 5:18*

John 4:24 really pulls it together well, God is a Spirit: and they that worship him must worship him in spirit and in truth.

It is quite simple. We cannot worship him in Spirit if we have not the Spirit. We can't be guided by the Spirit if we don't let him in!

This leads to another very interesting point.

God wants to fill you and not just surround you. In the old Testament we see examples of the Spirit of God coming upon people and anointing them to fulfil specific tasks. Here is an example:

*And the Lord spake unto Moses, saying,*
*See, I have called by name Bezaleel the son of Uri, the son of Hur, of the tribe of Judah:*
**And I have filled him with the spirit of God***, in wisdom, and in understanding, and in knowledge, and in all manner of workmanship,*
*To devise cunning works, to work in gold, and in silver, and in brass,*
*And in cutting of stones, to set them, and in carving of timber, to work in all manner of workmanship.*
*Exodus 31:1-5*

But in the book of Acts that we see the Spirit of God filling the Apostles for the first time.

*And when the day of Pentecost was fully come, they were all with one accord in one place.*
*And suddenly there came a sound from heaven as of a rushing mighty wind, and it filled all the house where they were sitting.*
*And there appeared unto them cloven tongues like as of fire, and it sat upon each of them.*
**And they were all filled with the Holy Ghost**, *and began to speak with other tongues, as the Spirit gave them utterance.*
*Acts 2:1-4*

This same act of the infilling is what Christ wants for you. Why be around when you can be inside?

For you to be truly apostolic (be as the apostles were), you must be filled with the Holy Spirit. Christ in me the hope of glory. Personally, for me there was too much evidence throughout the New Testament of its essential need, for one to dismiss it as something that was just for "special people". Still questioning? Try these

*For John truly baptized with water; but ye shall be baptized with the Holy Ghost not many days hence.*
*Acts 1:5*

*And, behold, I send the promise of my Father upon you: but tarry ye in the city of Jerusalem, until ye be endued with power from on high.*
*Luke 24:49*

*But ye shall receive power, after that the Holy Ghost is come upon you: and ye shall be witnesses unto me both in Jerusalem, and in all Judaea, and in Samaria, and unto the uttermost part of the earth.*
*Acts 1:8*

This Holy Spirit is real, and if you are to preach the gospel with power it is essential for you to be filled with it. Why else would Acts 1:8 be so explicit in its wording?

# 10
## How can I be filled?

How I can be filled with the Spirit of God?

As a preacher I am confident you have felt the Spirit of God around you, but as stated in previous chapters it is God's intention to now live inside you.

*He that believeth on me, as the scripture hath said, out of his belly shall flow rivers of living water.*
*John 7:38*

This is where the scripture really comes into its own. We see many outpourings of the Spirit in the book of Acts, which is the churches beginning, but there are several aspects that should be highlighted when analysing each of the events. Principles that can be used in individual lives or even corporately.

I would firstly say that there was a **longing**

They wanted more of the Spirit. They wanted to have Christ in them. They wanted to receive the promise of the father, so they waited. It is in the book of Acts 2 we see the consequence of them waiting. I am confident that at the very beginning there must have been more than just the 120 people that were sat in that upper room. It is known that approximately 500 people saw the resurrected Jesus Christ between his resurrection and his ascension. That should have been enough to convince them of the validity of his Godhead status. But after several days they are left with 120. I am sure they all had jobs to go to, they had things that could have taken precedent. But inside the 120 there was a longing for more of what God had promised, so they stayed.

I am reminded of the well-known worship song that states, "As did the deer pants for the water so my soul longs after you".

For you to be filled with the Spirit you must have a longing your heart to receive it.

You must also be receptive. I hope that I am wrong but there may be some of you reading this book who are annoyed at my comment of you needing to be filled with the spirit to be an effective preacher of the gospel. If you allow that offence to harbour in your heart, then it is highly unlikely you'll received from the Lord. But I encourage you to be receptive to the scripture that you're reading. That is why I have filled this book with so much scripture. So that it is not just my voice you are hearing but your belief is based upon the word of God that you are reading. After all, *"heaven and earth may pass away but the Lord's word shall never pass away"* (Matthew 24:35).

This that leads me onto the next point. We need to be informed. We need to know what is available to us for us to be able to reach out and grab the gift i.e. *the promise of the father'*.

As already mentioned in Acts 19 the disciples of John had no idea what the Holy Spirit was, and for this reason they had not received it. But by reading this book, I believe there is already a hunger in your heart for more, and now the word of God which has been written in this book enables you to understand what God has left for you to use. I encourage you to use the information and scripture that I have provided in this book to receive more from God and for yourself, so that you can teach others. More information can be found in Mark Hemus' book "Are you Really Saved?"

If we did not need to be filled with the Spirit of God, why on earth would he have told the disciples to *"wait for the promise of the father" (Acts 1:4)*, before they did anything? I submit that it was because he knew that they would be need more than just talent, more than just learning and head knowledge. God knew that they would need a mighty outpouring that only he could bring.

What happens when I am filled with the Holy Spirit?

When God fills you with the Holy Spirit it is one of the greatest experiences you will ever know. I personally was filled with the Spirit of God when I was nine years old and I remember it vividly up to this day.

Acts 10:48 mentions a number of things that happened when the household of Cornelius were filled with the Spirit. One of the key things is found in verse 46. It states that they heard them speak with tongues and magnify God.

The wonderful thing about this is that at this point Peter would have only heard Jewish people speak with tongues. But now Gentile people were being filled also.

As you read this book, and if your heart is pure, and if you desire to be filled with the Spirit as a preacher, I am confident that God can and will fill you. Because of him filling you as a sign you will speak with other tongues.

If you've never spoken with tongues before, this alone should give you a boost whilst reading this book. You are Christ's and His Spirit is around you. Now he's inside, **God wants you speak with tongues**. FACT.

In almost every instance in the book of Acts that we hear of the Spirit falling the evidence of this is that those who had received spoke in another language. From this we can submit that as a sign that the Spirit of God is inside we speak in another tongue/language. Paul calls it "tongues of angels" (1 Corinthians 13:1).

It could therefore be said that there are two types of tongues. The **initial evidence of speaking with tongues** found throughout Acts (Acts 2:1-4. Acts 10:45). And then **the gift of tongues** which comes with the gifts of the spirit found in 1 Corinthians 12.

In many instances you find that people who have not yet spoken in tongues dispute that tongues are needed, because... they don't speak in tongues. But those that speak with tongues are happy to declare that they are needed as a sign.

The point of stating all of this is not to get into a debate, but to clearly state that reader, God wants to fill you with the Holy Spirit so that you speak with tongues and can be effective as a preacher of the gospel.

**Why is this important**? I would submit to you that all of **this** adds to your tools as a preacher of the gospel. When you are praying in tongues you are praying the perfect will of God into a situation, into a message, into a platform of ministry. This is why Paul states in Romans 8:26-27

*Likewise, the Spirit also helpeth our infirmities: for we know not what we should pray for as we ought: but the Spirit itself maketh intercession for us with groanings which cannot be uttered.*
*And he that searcheth the hearts knoweth what is the mind of the Spirit, because he maketh intercession for the saints according to the will of God.*

Paul adds more wisdom in 1 Corinthians 14:4

**He who speaks in a tongue edifies himself**, *but he who prophesies edifies the church.*

I like to see it as though when we speak with tongues we are lifting weights in our Spirits to build up our spiritual man.

Therefore, in your prayer time, when looking to prepare a message, I strongly suggest that you spend time praying, speaking in tongues. Allow the presence of God to overshadow you after your time of worship and let God clean you out via the tongues of the Spirit.

Initially it may feel as though it is dry and that you are doing it in the "flesh". However, as you focus, and as your mind quietens, your spirit will begin to get in tune with God. I guarantee you the atmosphere will begin to feel completely different as God enters your room. All these experiences combine to make you a powerful preacher of the gospel.

Look at Peter, timid and ashamed at the crucifixion of our Lord and saviour Jesus Christ. Cursing out a little girl as they came around the fire to warm their hands. Look at the difference in this man as we see him again in the book of Acts 2. He is now full of the Holy Ghost and he stands and preaches a famous sermon based upon the prophet Joel. "In the last days says the Lord I will pour out my spirit upon all flesh".

Do not be surprised if this same life changing difference takes place in your life, for God wants to flow through you. Make up in your mind to be a channel of the Holy Spirit in your church, in your community and in your town.

## 11
## The Power of Fasting

Fasting isn't an element of Christianity that is mentioned very much at all now. It is almost a lost ancient art practiced only by extreme fundamentalists. I personally believe that the reason for this is quite simply because it is hard to do. It is not easy to deny the flesh. It's easier for me to listen to Christian growth messages on a podcast, than to go home and decide that I am going to humble myself before God and not eat for a season.

It is my encouragement to you that if as a preacher, you find time to fast then the power that is with you, while or after you do it, has the potential to multiply and catapult your ministry to a different level.

Let me remind you of the story of Jesus casting the demon out of the young boy. The disciples were unable to do it. They had tried everything and failed. And so, the boy's father brings his child to Jesus and Jesus subsequently casts the demon out of the boy. Afterwards the disciples asked Jesus how is it that they couldn't do it. The response from the master is now iconic

*This kind can come forth by nothing, but by prayer and **fasting**.*
*Mark 9:29*

There are some places you will not be able to go in your ministry unless you fast before God. Why? Because is fasting brings breakthrough. Fasting is me showing God how serious I am about a situation, so serious that I will weaken my body and strengthen my spirit. May I at this point submit to you that fasting is not just a Christian activity but there are other spiritual religions that understand the power of fasting and therefore do it also.

Fasting also makes them powerful in their own respective circles. It makes them sensitive to the spirit realm because their flesh is weakened.

Let's start from the beginning.

"Is this not the fast that I have chosen:
To loose the bonds of wickedness,
To undo the [c]heavy burdens,
To let the oppressed go free,
And that you break every yoke?
7 Is it not to share your bread with the hungry,
And that you bring to your house the poor who are [d]cast out;
When you see the naked, that you cover him,
And not hide yourself from your own flesh?
8 Then your light shall break forth like the morning,
Your healing shall spring forth speedily,
And your righteousness shall go before you;
The glory of the Lord shall be your rear guard.
9 Then you shall call, and the Lord will answer;
You shall cry, and He will say, 'Here I am.'

*Isaiah 58:6-9*

This is a stunning piece of scripture, and it is important for us to learn from the full chapter the kinds of fasts that do not please God, as well as discover those fasts that he desires. In the context of passage of scripture God's people were fasting in a way that he had not called for and therefore were not seeing any results. God states within the scripture that they were ignoring the way fasting should be conducted and they were treating it as an empty ritual.

In his book *Fasting for Spiritual Breakthrough* Elmer Towns states that there are four types of fasting that someone can use to come before God.

The first is that of the **normal fast**. This is going without food for a definite period of time. In a normal fast one will take in only liquids i.e. water or juice. The practicalities of this fast are that it can be from 1 day to 40 days. As always one should take extreme care with longer fasts.

There is then an **absolute fast** which allows no food or water at all. It goes without saying that this fast should be short. Moses when he went up to the mountain did an absolute fast, but this should never be attempted today. To be honest this type of fast over a long period of time would kill anyone without supernatural intervention. Be sure to test the spirit that tries to talk you into a 40 day fast even if it includes liquids.

There is then a **partial fast**. Within a partial fast one omits certain foods or is on a schedule that includes limited eating. I could be said that John the Baptist, on his diet of locusts and wild honey, was on a partial fast. As well as this, Daniel with his three friends took part in a partial fast, as the omitted certain foods from their diet. People who have hypoglycaemia and other diseases may consider this type of fast.

And lastly there is a **rotational fast** which consists of eating or removing certain families of foods for designated periods. Many Christians do this in times of lent

There are many physical benefits of fasting, as well as spiritual ones. *Russell* notes that just as the seventh day was designated a day of rest, so the very cells of our bodies need rest from food now and again. Doctors state that our bodies were designed to respond to sickness by fever but also by fasting. You will find that when you are ill the last thing that you want to do is to eat. God designed our bodies to heal themselves at the level of the cells. Therefore, fasting helps unclog the system and eliminate poisons.

As a preacher of the gospel there are different fasting options available to you. What I can tell you is that having fasted while preaching, or even before it, there is no feeling like it. There is liberty both physically and spiritually that cannot be compared with. It feels as though chains have been cut off and for the first time you realise the major difference between having a strong spirit and living in strong flesh.

There is a price that needs to be paid by anyone who wants to move to the next level in any area of life. Whether it be preaching, teaching or even secular activity. There is always a cost.

In the New Testament church fasting was an activity that took place as part of the course. The church fasted and prayed, and Peter was delivered from his prison. In Christendom nowadays, there are so many people who want the power and want the anointing but are not willing to pay the price. They aren't willing to do what it takes to get close to the Lord. The word of God is clear:

*But they that wait upon the Lord shall renew their strength; they shall mount up with wings as eagles;*

*they shall run, and not be weary; and they shall walk, and not faint.*
*Isaiah 40:31*

Ask yourself the question, are you willing to do what it takes, including fasting, to be an anointed preacher of the gospel? Because that is what it will take. Christ fasted 40 days. Moses fasted 40 days, Elijah fasted 40 days. There are some things that cannot be done without fasting.

If you are healthy and start from a healthy setting it is highly unlikely you will die from fasting. You should be able to go from anywhere between 1 and 7 days. I encourage you to add this fasting element to your sermon preparation. Add it to your lifestyle and see how God works in your life.

# 12
## Using the Spirit of God to Prepare what is to be delivered

In most cases when preparing a sermon, the Lord would have laid something on your heart, or allowed you to see something, or hear something that has triggered the need for a word to feed His people.

You will mull it over, just like a cow chewing the cud (as my Dad would say). You will be thinking of different aspects, maybe praying over them as you walk the dog, or drive the car. But then for most of us there will be a time where you must sit down and do your best to prepare in detail what God has put on your heart.

I live in a busy house with four girls including my wife. It can be very difficult to be in a place where there is stillness. Nevertheless, once you are still **inside** you can then begin to listen. I don't know if it's fashionable or not, but some people will put on music, someone will listen to preaching, watch YouTube videos. But I would encourage you to do whatever you feel comfortable with to get your mind where it is in line with God's spiritual realm.

This is where I also find praying in the spirit, i.e. praying in tongues a perfect companion. This God given activity, brings my body, mind and spirit into unison so that I can truly listen to what the Spirit has to say to me concerning the topics that have been laid on my heart. In many cases we are told that the wandering mind is a dangerous thing, however the Lord can sometimes use this to show you where he wants you to go in the sermon that you are writing.

As a side note, I feel it is imperative that this time is respected and fenced especially for those who are called to Pastor. The reason being is because when you are called to look after the Lords, flock one of the reasons you exist is to feed His Sheep. I'm reminded of the discourse between Jesus and Peter at the breakfast by the sea.

*So when they had eaten breakfast, Jesus said to Simon Peter, "Simon, son of [b]Jonah, do you love Me more than these?"*
*He said to Him, "Yes, Lord; You know that I love You."*
*He said to him,* **"Feed My lambs."**
*He said to him again a second time, "Simon, son of Jonah, do you love Me?"*
*He said to Him, "Yes, Lord; You know that I love You."*
*He said to him,* **"Tend My sheep."**
*He said to him the third time, "Simon, son of Jonah, do you love Me?" Peter was grieved because He said to him the third time, "Do you love Me?"*

*And he said to Him, "Lord, You know all things; You know that I love You."*
*Jesus said to him,* ***"Feed My sheep.***
*John 21:15-17*

At this point as you kneel, pace or sit at your desk I would encourage you to spend some time thinking about this conversation between Peter and our Lord. Mediate on the magnitude of the responsibility that God has put on you to feed His sheep.

Also, consider prayerfully that fact that when you feed his sheep you are declaring your love for him.

This revelation and scripture changed the way I approached preparing my sermons. After years of just writing notes and then going by the seat of my pants, praying that the Spirit would pick up a note, I now try and prepare a sermon in the way a chef would prepare a meal, understanding the content is more important than hype.

Ask yourself:
1. How can I feed the women and men of God today?
2. What does God want me to say to His church today that will cause them to grow?

So, pray in tongues, loud or low but completely lose yourself in God for a season and allow him to impress things on your heart. Let him show you pictures, and then begin to write notes on what you see and what you feel. This is truly walking in the spirit. Then begin to write your sermon.

I cannot say that I have ever heard the voice of God out of heaven, (In a Jesus at his baptism type manner) telling me exactly what I need to preach. But what I can say is that I have had such strong impressions on my heart concerning subjects and topics that as I would write it felt like the pen was being held by God himself. And as that tears would roll down my face I would know for sure that what I was about to deliver to the people of God was not from me but 100% from the Lord.

As you write.

I have always believed that practical advice is most of the time better to understand and apply than when one uses churchy, spiritual speak. Therefore, I will be as transparent as I can in this area.

There were times where my notes would literally be 4 sides of A4 covered in bullet points. There would also be times where I would write a whole sermon verbatim. I could end up with 24 pages of A4 size 16 font. As the years have gone by I have changed, and therefore my preparation techniques changed. Therefore, I will share with you now, a system has been a real blessing to me. The system is that of **dictation.**

There are many dictating software's available on the market. Truthfully speaking, I am dictating this book right now. But as for preparing, my process is now to open my Bible, have my references around me and then preach to a dictation application on my phone. It then means that every word that I speak it is written down and I can flow freely from whatever God may lay on my heart. I cannot stress the importance of being able to flow as you prepare your message.

It is my experience that if I am unable to flow in preparation then most of the time what I have isn't what God has for that specific time, or I'm not going along the lines the Lord would have me to travel. When what I have is directly from the Throne of Grace it is as though there is oil flowing through the gears of my heart and mind. However, I must state that this is only my personal experience.

After I have completed writing my sermon I will then go through it and edit it into a preach-able format.

I have found that this way of preparing a gospel message is extremely efficient. It really works well for my sermon preparation skill-set. I encourage you to try it and see how it fits you.

A Glimpse of the Gifts

I have had the opportunity to be used in the Gifts of the Spirit on many occasions. These include, the word of wisdom, word of knowledge and the gift of prophecy. I would submit to you that when preparing a sermon, it is almost as though the spirit of prophecy rests upon you when writing. Following on from this, it could be said that preaching of itself is a prophetic act. So, I encourage you to bare this in mind as you prepare your powerful gospel message.

## 13
## Preach it – Delivery

*"We are so pleased to have Rev... here with us tonight. He is truly a man of God and we are looking forward to a tremendous move of the Spirit this evening..."*. No pressure there then!

I'm sure we all get those delivery butterflies at some point. The final moments before we are going up to deliver a message can be the most nerve wracking.

What shall I say to link one part of the service to the other? How shall I open and link it through to my text? Even questions such as, do I need the toilet? Am I going to be sick? Is this message even from the Lord or religious flesh? come through the mind. All of this is normal.

But then it is time for you to go up and deliver what God has given to you. All the prayer, all the fasting, all the deliberation over texts, Hebrew, Greek, all these things now have to be presented in a way that the people of God can digest and apply it to their lives. Over to you preacher man!

The best way for me to break down the delivery of a sermon is by dividing it into a **practical** element and a spiritual element.

Practical.

When you are preaching, you are not necessarily sharing you are delivering. You are declaring the word of God expecting no come back, just agreement.

Like a solicitor, barrister or attorney delivering their final speech, the speech that will close the case, it is with this authority you must declare what God has given you. Deliver it firmly and with passion. Do not babble as though you are unsure of yourself but be sure of what God has given you. Deliver with confidence that which you have prayed and laboured over.

Be clear. Take your time. If you feel as though you need to reiterate points, do so, so that they understand. Let them hang on every word, because it's not coming from you it is coming from the King of Kings.

If while you are preaching memories of relevant stories come to mind, if you are sure that you can remember the whole story then deliver it. Many times, in my own ministry, stories have come to mind when not part of my notes. I have subsequently delivered these stories because the Spirit of God highlighted them, and they end up being a key element of the sermon that has blessed people.

So, put your shoulders back and give it. Declare it with everything you have. As you do this you'll feel the presence of God overshadow you and you'll know for a surety that he is with you as you deliver the word. Preach it!

Spiritual

The best way that I can describe the spiritual journey whilst delivering a message is that of a surfer looking for a wave to catch. Don't get me wrong, what you have at this stage of the process has been prayed over and is still anointed. The bottom line is that it is indeed the word of God.

However, in most cases there will be times where after delivering a statement, or story you will feel the Spirit of God lean on what has been stated. Almost like a "Hint of the Spirit", and it is at this time that I encourage you to trust the revelation that God begins to pour out of your mouth.

Go with how you are feeling (within reason), go with what God impresses on your heart and just deliver it. Forget your notes for that second and ride the wave until you feel it no longer and then go back to your notes.

After over 20 years of preaching I have found that generally it is in these periods of spiritual surfing the most poignant points are made. When people come up to me afterwards and tell me that a specific point was "exactly what they needed in that situation", in most cases it was stated during a "surfing period" where I went with the *rhema* word. It is important to realise that it is in these periods that God can use the word of knowledge without you even realising that you are moving in the Gifts of the Spirit. This is truly walking in the spirit.

Now many people feel different ways as they physically deliver the word of God. I personally have felt the Holy Ghost as a fire with tingling in my hands. In most cases it feels as though oil has been poured into the foundation of my message. Suddenly, I am in a flow, and with that flow comes scripture and insight that I had previously learned but now is being brought to the forefront. Like a student in the middle of an exam, all the studying that has been done throughout my life now comes to memory, brought there by the Holy Ghost.

As a side note, this is why it is so important that we read the bible every day, even if we don't understand parts of it. This is why it's important that we spend time in prayer, because when I read my Bible it allows me to have something to draw from in those moments of delivery. When I have experience in prayer and understand what it is to be in presence of the Lord, I can quickly recognise when His anointing comes during delivery of a message. This is where God wants you to be.

What must be said is that in all these preaching components the Spirit is subject to the prophet.

*The spirits of prophets are subject to the control of prophets*
*1 Corinthians 14:32*

It is subject to you and everything must be done with decency and in order. You are responsible for what comes out of your mouth, anointed and not anointed. It is my sincere belief that the Church of God has come to harm from people who have stated that they *"couldn't not stop it was the spirit of God inside of them,"* when in fact this is not scriptural at all.

God expects the preacher of the gospel to use wisdom in all things, so I encourage you to use the Holy Spirit along with faith and wisdom to declare the message God has given to you both prepared beforehand and through spontaneous revelation.

## 14
## Moving in the Holy Ghost

So, you have given it your all. You have declared what God gave to you with passion and authority. In the places where you felt the "wave" you rode it. The presence of God is now strong in the sanctuary and God is wanting to move among His people…

Now what?

I would submit to you that it is this moment all your preparation has been building up to. All the studying, all the fasting, all the late nights, all the worrying, all the nervousness has led to this point. It is time for God to do what only he can do. You just need to make sure you know what he wants to do.

It is my belief that because many people are unsure of how to operate with the Holy Spirit, God is frustrated that he cannot get through to His people, primarily because of fear on behalf of the preacher. In the light of this in this chapter I will share with you some practical hints that will give you confidence to move forward and create avenues for God to touch people, whether it be at an altar call or even as they are in their pews. What I share with you has completely changed my life and I pray that it would completely change yours also, as you use it to find the will of God for that 'specific moment', so that His people can be blessed.

Right and Left

It was while at a training course in Riga Latvia (www.rbdna.org) that I was introduced to the left-hand and right-hand biblical principle. Follow me carefully and it will all make sense.

This truth begins when Moses has a discussion with his Father-in-Law Jethro.

*And it came to pass on the morrow, that Moses sat to judge the people: and the people stood by Moses from the morning unto the evening.*

*And when Moses' father in law saw all that he did to the people, he said, What is this thing that thou doest to the people? why sittest thou thyself alone, and all the people stand by thee from morning unto even?*

*And Moses said unto his father in law, Because the people come unto me to enquire of God:*

*When they have a matter, they come unto me; and I judge between one and another, and I do make them know the statutes of God, and his laws.*

*And Moses' father in law said unto him, The thing that thou doest is not good.*

*Thou wilt surely wear away, both thou, and this people that is with thee: for this thing is too heavy for thee; thou art not able to perform it thyself alone.*

*Hearken now unto my voice, **I will give thee counsel**, and God shall be with thee: Be thou for the people to God-ward, that thou mayest bring the causes unto God:*
*Exodus 18:13-19*

Like most of us Pastors, in this scripture Moses is doing way too much and is going to burn himself out. So, Jethro states that if he continues he will "wear away". Jethro then states here let me give you **counsel** so that you can manage these people more efficiently. The Hebrew word for counsel is where we get our word "Blueprint". Jethro is saying, let me give you the blueprint on how to manage what is believed to be over 2 million people.

The blue print looked like what we see below.

| **Left Side** | **Moses** | **Right Side** |
|---|---|---|
| **Aaron** | | **Joshua** |
| Law | | Military |

| | |
|:---:|:---:|
| Priest | Kings |
| Worship | Conquerors |
| Character | Power |
| Gabriel | Michael |
| Truth | Spirit |

On the right-hand side they had the warlords headed by Joshua.
On the left-hand side they had the priesthood headed by Aaron.

Underneath that they had captains/priests over thousands
Captains/priests over hundreds
Captains/priests over tens

Another word for captains is Pastor. So organised was the system that any point a horn could be blown, and the structure would fall into place, ready for war or worship.

(For further information read through the rest of Exodus 18 or contact Revival By Design at www.rbdna.org)

As you can see from the diagram, this structure of left-hand and right-hand is something that we begin see on a regular basis throughout the Bible.

In addition to this if you look at spiritual elements you will also see how everything falls into place. We are called to be Kings(right) and Priest (left), or when we look at the Lord's archangels there is Gabriel who is a ministering spirit (left) and Michael who is known as the Lords angel responsible for warfare (right).

The element that causes the right-hand side and left-hand side to be balanced is that of **brokenness** before God. Nevertheless, what is clear from scripture and Christian living throughout the ages is that both are needed alongside brokenness. For the church to be effective we cannot help one side without the other.

Division of Aaron (Left).

If we refer to the conversation that Jethro has with Moses, it is at this stage that the priesthood that represents the law is first installed. It is through this division that the Lord dealt with character of the people and the issue of sacrifice. The priesthood dealt with discipline and explained that there was a way to come to God. It had very much to do with the word. We know from John 17:17 that His word is truth.

We know that there are many who are just interested in the demonstration and power of God without knowing him. But true worship comes from knowing him. Paul cries in Philippians 3:10:
*That I may* **know him**, *and the power of his resurrection, and the fellowship of his sufferings, being made conformable unto his death*

Part of living in the left-hand side calls from consecration. Romans 12:1-2

*I beseech you therefore, brethren, by the mercies of God, that ye present your bodies a living sacrifice, holy, acceptable unto God, which is your reasonable service.*
*And be not conformed to this world: but be ye transformed by the renewing of your mind, that ye may prove what is that good, and acceptable, and perfect, will of God.*

Nevertheless, it is dangerous to have just a priesthood focused life with no balance.
If someone is imbalanced in this area, they can become like the Pharisees of Jesus 'day. Very judgemental and legalistic. The scripture that comes to mind is found in 2 Corinthians 3:6.

*Who also hath made us able ministers of the new testament; not of the letter, but of the spirit:* **for the letter killeth, but the spirit giveth life**.

People can get so righteous in their doctrine or in their way of living before God that it replaces God himself. Nevertheless, the priesthood (left-side) is still essential for a balanced ministry.

Stay with me, I'm going somewhere…

## The Division of Joshua (Right)

We call this area the right-hand side or the Spirit side. In this area the Lord taught Joshua the power of praise. It was all about victory and triumph. If we remember the walls of Jericho it was because of the shout that the walls came down.

In the book of Chronicles, the story of Jehoshaphat comes to mind. We read that when he put the singers in front of the army God came down and destroyed the enemy. There was a great miracle that took place that day and it was through the power of praise.

I would classify the baptism of the Holy Ghost is one of the greatest miracles that we see daily. God filling someone with the spirit and them speaking with another language that they have not been taught is nothing short of miraculous. In every instance that the power of God falls upon them they speak out. They make a sound and they rejoice, they go to right side, spiritually speaking.

However, as with the priesthood it is easy for someone to become imbalanced dwelling only on the right. They enjoy the miracles, signs and wonders but do not really know the God from whom all these gifts flow. This is why the scripture states the following:

*Not everyone that saith unto me, Lord, Lord, shall enter into the kingdom of heaven; but he that doeth the will of my Father which is in heaven.*

*Many will say to me in that day, Lord, Lord, have we not prophesied in thy name? and in thy name have cast out devils? and in thy name done many wonderful works?*

*And then will I profess unto them, I never knew you: depart from me, ye that work iniquity.*

Matthew 7:21-23

Therefore, we do need each side to be able to move effectively in the Spirit. As preachers we must be able to recognise each side during a service after we have ministered. In most cases you will be able to sense it even before you have finished. Interestingly there have been many times where I was expecting the end of the sermon to be a tremendous shout and God has caused a holy hush to enter the fray (left side). Likewise, there have been times where I was expecting an altar call where people would come and dedicate their lives to the Christ and it has finished with a shout of victory and of praise with people receiving the gift of the Holy Spirit (right side)

We know that the Gifts of the Spirit are all activated according to the will of God however, when you finish your sermon, or even in the middle of your sermon it is important for us to know what God is wanting to do, i.e. which gifts are most likely to be activated depending on the atmosphere.

This is where 'Hints of the Spirit' come into their own.

Hints of the spirit

The following generalities are simply what I have experienced during my time preaching. That being said, God can always do what he wants to do when he wants to do it.

Divers tongues and the interpretation of tongues are gifts that are generally indicated by a Holy

Hush. In layman's terms, this is when after ministering a stillness comes across the congregation. At this point God is giving you a hint showing you that he wants to speak to his people. (left side)

When the gift of prophecy operates in many cases but not exclusively there is more of a spirit of praise (left side) that comes across the auditorium before the hush. Subsequently the way that the word is declared through the prophetic vessel is purposeful, passionate and prophetic.

When there is a great authority that you feel in your spirit after you have ministered be aware that it is likely the gift of faith is also available (right side).

The gifts of healing are sometimes indicated by feeling of compassion, and this can be also coupled with intercession. It could have been a case that you have experienced this before in a prayer meeting. Be aware that if there are any sick among you this could be an opportunity for the gifts of healing to be in operation. When we see Jesus ministering to the sick in the gospels the phrase "moved with compassion" is almost always used, this is no mere coincidence (left side).

In over 20 years of preaching ministry I have found that there is normally a victory shout, that enters the sanctuary when miracles are just about to happen so be aware of this feeling in your spirit after or while you are preaching. It may even happen whilst you are sharing stories to build faith (right side).

The last hint I would give is that of the words of wisdom and knowledge being present during quiet seasons or if there is opportunity for one off speech or one-to-one engagement (left side). There would be a quietness in your spirit so that you can hear from God and therefore minister to those in need

Use these hints to allow you to move in the spirit. For me it took me sometime to trust what I felt. However, just like anything in life, the more you do it the easier it becomes and the more sensitive you become.

I also find that if indeed I have just come off a fast or I am in the middle of the fast then my spiritual sensitivity becomes heightened and it is easier for me to distinguish what God is doing at any point in time.

I'll conclude this section my reiterating that as Preachers we must have both spirit (right) and truth (left). And the only thing that keeps is balanced is brokenness before God.

*And they that are Christ's have crucified the flesh with the affections and lusts.*
*If we live in the Spirit, let us also walk in the Spirit.*
*Galatians 5:24-25,*

*If ye abide in me, and my words abide in you, ye shall ask what ye will, and it shall be done unto you.*
*John 15:7*

# 15
# Conclusion

I honestly believe that now more than ever before is the time for the true preachers of the gospel stand and declare the pure word of God like never before. It's time to declare the word with passion and an anointing that breaks the yoke.

There are many people who attract itching ears, mix scripture with a positive thinking ethos and self-development jargon. Yes, I admit that there will be some crossover because the bible is our basis on how to live, however, I do believe that instead of the diluted gospel that we sometimes find across our television screens and in our pulpits, God is looking for a preacher that will preach the undiluted, powerful and effective gospel in this generation.

I often think of John the Baptist and what a mighty preacher he would have been. To decide to go out into the wilderness and preach the gospel. So powerful was this man's preaching that it caused people to come out of the city to listen to him. It is this type of anointing that is needed today to break the yoke of sin upon our generation and set the captives free.

God is looking for men and women that will stand upon their watch and declare that Jesus is alive and that his word is true. He is looking for people who preach hope and declare that His Kingdom is at hand.

Now is not the time to hang on until Jesus comes, but it is truly the time to declare the Kingdom of God and to let the preaching of the word be followed by miracles, signs and wonders.

I encourage you to use the principals mentioned in this book take you to new place with God. Let them set alight your faith and be part of the foundation that you build your ministry upon. Realise that in the words of Mordechai *"you were brought to the kingdom for such at time as this"*. So, preach it. Preach it until revival happens in your city. Preach it until the faith level in your area is transformed and men and women see and experience Jesus Christ.

This is how you preach the gospel with power.

Bonus

Simply as a 'thank you' for purchasing this book I would like to give you my ebook titled "When Kingdoms Collide – *How to pray the kingdom of God into your life and see things happen*" **FREE of charge.**

In addition to this, you will receive access to our newsletter that will update you weekly regarding new teaching and offers available.

Please claim your free copy here at https://bit.ly/2ycGFTh

If you enjoyed the book, please feel free to bless us by leaving a review at https://amzn.to/2zSkCn1

Printed in the USA
CPSIA information can be obtained
at www.ICGtesting.com
LVHW011944161123
764168LV00013B/74